CLIMATE CHANGE AND THE POLAR REGIONS

BY MICHAEL BURGAN

CLIMATE CHANGE AND THE POLAR REGIONS

BY MICHAEL BURGAN

MASON CREST

Mason Crest
450 Parkway Drive, Suite D
Broomall, PA 19008
www.masoncrest.com

Printed and bound in the United States of America.

First printing
1 3 5 7 9 8 6 4 2

Series ISBN: 978-1-4222-3863-9
ISBN: 978-1-4222-3868-4
ebook ISBN: 978-1-4222-7923-6

Library of Congress Cataloging-in-Publication Data on file with the publisher.

Developed and Produced by Shoreline Publishing Group.
Developmental Editor: James Buckley, Jr.
Design: Tom Carling, Carling Design Inc.
Production: Sandy Gordon
www.shorelinepublishing.com
Front cover: Denis Burdin/Dreamstime.com

QR Codes disclaimer:

CONTENTS

Key Icons to Look For

Words to Understand: These words with their easy-to-understand definitions will increase the reader's understanding of the text, while building vocabulary skills.

Sidebars: This boxed material within the main text allows readers to build knowledge, gain insights, explore possibilities, and broaden their perspectives by weaving together additional information to provide realistic and holistic perspectives.

Educational Videos: Readers can view videos by scanning our QR codes, providing them with additional educational content to supplement the text. Examples include news coverage, moments in history, speeches, iconic sports moments, and much more!

Text-Dependent Questions: These questions send the reader back to the text for more careful attention to the evidence presented here.

Research Projects: Readers are pointed toward areas of further inquiry connected to each chapter. Suggestions are provided for projects that encourage deeper research and analysis.

Series Glossary of Key Terms: This back-of-the-book glossary contains terminology used throughout this series. Words found here increase the reader's ability to read and comprehend higher-level books and articles in this field.

INTRODUCTION

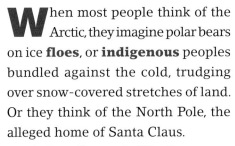

Words to Understand

extracting   removing something

floes   large sheets of floating ice

glaciers   large masses of ice that move slowly over land

indigenous   native to a particular region

lichen   a plant-like structure made up of fungus and another life form

meteorologists   scientists who study the climate and make predictions about the weather

When most people think of the Arctic, they imagine polar bears on ice **floes**, or **indigenous** peoples bundled against the cold, trudging over snow-covered stretches of land. Or they think of the North Pole, the alleged home of Santa Claus.

At the other end of Earth, an even colder and harsher climate defines Antarctica, a continent larger than the United States and surrounded by the Southern Ocean. Antarctica is the planet's coldest, driest, and windiest continent. Winds during blizzards can reach 200 miles (321 km) per hour, and in places the ice is more than one mile (1.6 km) thick. In his 2003 book *The Ice*, historian Stephen Pyne wrote

that "ice is the beginning of Antarctica and ice is its end." During the winter, ice that forms along its coasts nearly doubles the continent's size. Unlike the Arctic, no one lived in Antarctica before scientists set up research bases during the 20th century. At one of those bases, the temperature once plunged to -129°F (-89.4°C)—the coldest temperature ever recorded on Earth.

All the ice and snow in the world's polar regions, though, doesn't mean they lack some warmth. During the summer, thanks to Earth's tilt and its orbit around the sun, the days are long. Parts of the Arctic warm enough to blossom with small plants, and wildlife roams over flat, mostly treeless plains called tundras. Antarctica, meanwhile, lacks plants such as shrubs or trees, though it does have two types of flowering plants and algae, moss, and **lichen**. Temperatures during its summer months rise along the coasts to above freezing. Sometimes they even reach the 50s °F (10s °C)—a heat wave by Antarctic standards.

The natural, seasonal warming of the polar regions, however, does not explain some extreme changes scientists have detected in those environments. For several decades, the polar regions have been feeling the effects of climate change, which is also sometimes called global warming. Temperatures across the planet have steadily risen, and in 2014 **meteorologists** saw the highest average global temperatures ever recorded. The next year was even hotter. In 2016, the National Aeronautics and Space Administration (NASA) reported that 15 of the 16 hottest years ever recorded occurred during the 21st century. How does this extreme warming trend affect the polar regions? In Antarctica, for example, the warming

of the Southern Ocean has led to the melting of **glaciers** and ice sheets. In the Arctic, higher temperatures have made it harder for polar bears to hunt their traditional prey and the vast ice sheets have started to crack or disappear.

Nearly every scientist who has looked at this problem agrees that climate change is in part fueled by human activity. People have shaped the environments of the polar regions before, whether through hunting land or sea animals or, more recently, **extracting** natural resources such as oil. But the effects of climate change could be more drastic for the polar regions than anything in the past. In a few small cases, it could have a positive impact. Indigenous people of the Arctic might be able to raise new crops or create jobs by digging for minerals. Overall, though, the warming of the polar regions threatens wildlife and the health of other parts of the planet on a local and a global scale. Here's a closer look at how climate change does and will continue to affect Earth's polar regions.

The polar regions include enormous amounts of the Earth's freshwater, most of it in the form of huge floes and icebergs.

Changes at the End of the Earth

Words to Understand

atmosphere   the layer of gases that surrounds Earth

fossil fuels   fuels such as natural gas and oil that formed in the ground millions of years ago from dead, rotting plants and animals

industrialization   the large-scale process of using machines powered by fossil fuels to make goods in factories

models   numbers or ideas that describe how something could develop in the future

During the past two decades, stories on climate change have filled the news, as scientists study its causes and what it could mean for Earth's future. Climate change is not new; what does seem to be new is the *rate* at which temperatures are rising and the effects it could have on billions of people.

The planet has had cycles of warming and cooling going back millions of years, due to slight variations in Earth's orbit around the sun. Cool periods of the past produced what are called ice ages, when massive glaciers like those in the polar regions covered much more of Earth's Northern Hemisphere. About 20,000 years ago, as the last Ice Age was ending, the glaciers started melting in North America and other parts of the world. The process lasted for about 10,000 years. Before the glaciers melted, ice sheets in North America reached as far south as what is now Illinois.

Scientists believe that the gas carbon dioxide (CO_2) and the subsequent changes in Earth's orbit played a part in ending the last ice age. As the planet slowly warmed, CO_2 stored deep in the Southern Ocean around Antarctica was released into the **atmosphere**. This gas has been called a greenhouse gas, because when it goes into the atmosphere it traps heat close to Earth's surface while still letting in light. A greenhouse used to raise plants does the same thing—it lets in sunlight and keeps the sun's heat inside the building.

Many greenhouse gases occur naturally, and during the 19th century, scientists began to understand that a "greenhouse effect" explained some rise in temperature on Earth. The greenhouse effect has a positive side, as the warmth it generates allowed early humans to spread out around the globe and for plants to grow. Problems began to arise, however, over the last few centuries. Inventors created such things as the steam engine, gas-powered vehicles, and electrical power plants, which

Greenhouse gases

The heat of radiation from the sun (yellow) hits the Earth. The rise in greenhouse gases traps more and more of the reflected heat off the Earth (red).

relied on **fossil fuels** to run. When they burn, these fuels produce CO_2 and other greenhouse gases. Other human activity, such as raising more livestock and using chemical fertilizers, also released more of those gases. During the 20th century, some researchers began to realize that temperatures were rising around the Earth as the amount of greenhouse gases increased. Human activity was increasing the greenhouse effect and creating a dangerous change in the climate.

An Important Curve

Trained as a chemist, Charles David Keeling had an early interest in studying carbon dioxide in the atmosphere. He built his own device to measure it and then began collecting samples around the globe. He wanted to try to collect data that would test the idea that human activity was raising CO_2 levels. That led to his work in Antarctica and Hawaii, which showed the levels were rising from year to year, though within a given year CO_2 levels rise and fall. Keeling's and others' research later showed the oceans were not able to absorb all the CO_2 produced. Working at the Scripps Institute of Oceanography for almost 50 years, Keeling amassed a huge amount of information on rising CO_2 levels. The graphed results of what he measured in Hawaii over the decades are known as the Keeling Curve (right). The curve is considered so important to science that a copy of it is carved into the wall of the National Academy of Sciences in Washington, D.C.

Studying Climate Change in the Polar Regions

Research into CO_2 levels began during the 1950s. The effort received a push from the International Geophysical Year (IGY), which began in 1957. During the IGY, scientists from more than 60 countries studied such topics as gravity, global weather patterns, the oceans, and earthquakes. The effort was based on earlier international efforts to study the polar regions, and Antarctica was a major focus of the IGY. A young scientist named Charles David Keeling

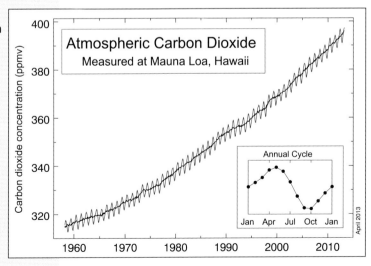

This Canadian scientist is readying a machine that will drill down into the thick ice and retrieve a core sample that can show climate change over time.

set up measuring devices on Hawaii's Mauna Loa volcano and at the Little America navy base in Antarctica. This was part of a long-range project to measure changes in CO_2 levels. By 1960, Keeling had hard evidence from the Antarctica site that CO_2 levels were rising.

The IGY led to increased interest in studying the polar regions as well as the signing of the Antarctic Treaty. The 12 nations that had carried out research on the continent pledged to pursue more scientific study there and share their results. The countries also agreed to use Antarctica "for peaceful purposes only." Today, more than 50 nations have signed the treaty.

In the decades that followed the IGY, researchers worked in both polar regions to try to understand changes in Earth's climate. Some of the key information came from ice cores—samples of ice drilled out of glaciers and ice sheets. A single ice core can be more than one mile (1.6 km) deep and contain information from Earth's atmosphere as much as 800,000 years old as bubbles of ancient air were trapped in the ice. That air gives scientists information about levels of CO_2 and other greenhouse gases from the distant past.

Ice cores from Antarctica seemed to show the role of **industrialization** in increasing the amount of CO_2 in the

The Climate Change Debate

In recent years, NASA has played a large role in researching and discussing climate change. Almost 30 years ago, one of its scientists, John Hansen, helped inform the public about the human role in climate change. Today, NASA reports that 97 percent of scientists who study the climate agree that the globe is warming and that human activity plays a part. Some US politicians, however, say there is no proof that the warming is taking place as fast as some experts say, or is even happening at all. Other climate change deniers note the planet's historical pattern of warming and cooling. They do not think human activity is fueling a faster-than-usual temperature rise. President Donald Trump was clear on his views in an interview with CNN: "I don't believe in climate change," though he later somewhat moderated that view. Senator James Inhofe, who is on the Senate's Committee on Environment and Public Works, wrote a book calling climate change *The Greatest Hoax*.

Many deniers fear that steps needed to reduce the production of CO_2, such as using less oil and coal, could force some companies out of business. But most scientists believe the world must take steps to reduce greenhouse gases. In an interview with *Yale Environment 360* in 2016, Hansen said: "No one expected that governments would react immediately when it was still just based on simple **models** 40 years ago, but now, it's not just [computer] models. We can see what's happening."

The burning of fossil fuels by industry, cars, trucks, ships, and more has rapidly and greatly changed the atmosphere around the Earth, with ongoing consequences.

atmosphere. The amount of CO_2 trapped in the cores remained constant for almost one thousand years before the 19th century. Since then, however, with the increased burning of fossil fuels, the amount of CO_2 in the atmosphere has increased by almost 40 percent. Information gathered from other cores suggests that the overall amount of CO_2 and the speed at which it's increasing in the atmosphere are unlike anything Earth has experienced for at least 800,000 years. The ice cores show a similar recent increase in the amount of methane in the atmosphere. Like CO_2 methane is a common greenhouse gas.

Other research with ice cores has allowed scientists to use the trapped air to estimate what temperatures were like on Earth over time. They have seen a clear connection—a rise in CO_2 levels and warming temperatures have historically happened at the same time. The results don't necessarily mean that one caused the other, but the connection suggests a relationship between temperature and CO_2 levels.

Scientists are working hard to understand how climate change is affecting both polar regions. In 2013, researcher Charles Miller told NASA that "the Arctic is critical to understanding global

One effect of warming ocean temperatures is an increase in the early breakup of pack ice in the polar regions, which can have negative effects on wildlife.

climate…Looking at the Arctic is like looking at the canary in the coal mine for the entire Earth system."

Coal miners once took canaries with them to warn if deadly gases were filling a mine. The canary would die before the gas affected the miners, giving them time to flee. Miller and others see the changes in the polar regions as doing something similar today. They are warning us about possible dangers ahead for the whole planet. As early as 1999, the US Arctic Research Commission saw that "change in the Arctic may play a substantial role in climate change throughout the globe."

 # Text-Dependent Questions:

1. What change in Earth's atmosphere did the Keeling Curve record?

2. Why are CO_2 and methane referred to as "greenhouse gases"?

3. What kind if information can ice cores from Greenland and Antarctica reveal?

 # Research Project

Retreating glaciers have shaped the land in parts of the world. Use the Internet to find out what kind of changes they can make on Earth's surface.

This man is from the Buryat people of northern Russia. The Buryats are one of dozens of native populations whose lives will be affected by climate change.

The Arctic and Climate Change

For thousands of years, indigenous peoples of Earth's most northerly regions have found a way to live in the cold climate of the Arctic. In more recent centuries, European explorers and then settlers came to the region. Today, at least eight nations lay claim to parts of the Arctic, which includes the Arctic Ocean and part of the North Atlantic Ocean.

In 1999, some US scientists predicted that global climate change could have its most dramatic effects in the Arctic. Residents across the region don't need scientists to tell them that

The impact of climate change on polar bears—a shrinking hunting ground, difficulty crossing usually ice-covered water, and other factors—has drawn world attention.

something is happening to the Arctic because of warming temperatures. In Nome, Alaska, Richard Beneville looked out his living room window in 2016 and saw open water where in the past he saw ice. Since the early 2000s, he told National Public Radio, the length of time that the ice shut down Nome's port each year has decreased by about two months. He added, "Our ice is about a third as thick as it used to be." Beneville had no doubt that climate change in the Arctic is real.

What the science shows is that over the last 50 years, average temperatures have risen much faster in Alaska than in the continental United States. That has led to the melting of billions of tons of glacial ice every year. Across the Arctic, temperatures are rising twice as fast as in the rest of the world.

The media often talks about the fate of polar bears as the Arctic warms. The bears use floating sea ice as a base to catch their main source of food, seals. As the ice melts, the bears find it harder to hunt. While they can get some of the nutrition they need from land-based foods, they are struggling to survive. But climate change in the Arctic affects the people who live there as well.

Affect on People

That point is often made by the indigenous Arctic peoples. Several dozen different groups live in the Arctic, representing about 10 percent of the approximately four million Arctic residents. One of those groups is the Sami of northern Sweden, Norway, Finland, and Russia's Kola Peninsula. The Sami are famous for raising reindeer, and their language gave us the English word *tundra*. They live with the effects of global warming every day, and they worry that the rest of the world is not devoting enough attention to climate change in the Arctic.

The Paris Climate Change Agreement

Since 1992, nations around the world have met to discuss climate change and how to slow it. In December 2015, representatives from 195 countries met for the Paris Climate Conference. In the end, they agreed to cut greenhouse gas **emissions** so that Earth will not warm more than 3.6°F (2°C) above what global temperatures were before the world began to industrialize. If the planet warms more than that, many scientists predict an even greater rise in sea levels than what the world is experiencing now. Other impacts of greater global warming include more severe droughts and stronger storms. Signing the Paris Agreement, however, did not mean a country would actually pass laws or make other changes to lower greenhouse gas emissions. For example, Rodrigo Duterte, president of the Philippines, said in 2016 that his country would not honor the agreement while he was in office. In the United States, the Republican Party also said it rejected the agreement. In late 2016, China said it had approved the agreement, however, giving hope to other signers.

Many Sami, along with other indigenous people, were disappointed that the 2015 Paris Agreement on climate change seemed to ignore the role indigenous people can play in addressing the issue. Josefina Skerk, a Sami political leader in Sweden, told Radio Canada International in 2015 that world leaders need to respect the knowledge the indigenous people have about their region. She said the people know the Arctic "like you would know a family member." The indigenous people, for example, can see changes in how ice forms or in the habits of Arctic wildlife before scientists do. Drawing on that knowledge can perhaps both soften the effects of climate change and preserve the indigenous peoples' traditional cultures.

Rapidly Melting Ice

The situation polar bears face points out one of the major results of climate change in the Arctic: the melting of sea ice. As the ice melts in both polar regions, the world's oceans rise from the

*Prime Minister Justin Trudeau of Canada was one of many world leaders who
signed the 2016 Paris Agreement on Climate Change.*

increase in water. Rising ocean levels eventually could threaten
many cities that sit at or near sea level. In the worst-case scenario,
even if global temperatures simply remain where they are now,
the seas could rise dozens of feet over the next few centuries.

One focus of the melting sea ice is Greenland. The world's
largest island is under Danish control and is mostly covered
with ice. If all the ice there melted, the seas could rise almost 20

Scientists are carefully studying the lands and waters of Greenland, such as Scorebysund here, to track the effects of climate change.

feet. Already, between 1995 and 2010, Greenland's ice melt has added more than 3,000 billion tons of freshwater to the ocean. Then research released in 2016 showed that one trillion more tons melted between 2011 and 2014. Greenland still has large areas of glaciers and ice sheets, but temperatures there are rising, and ice is melting faster than it did in the past. In April 2016, researchers saw that more of the ice was melting across the island than they had recorded during previous Aprils. As reported in *Climate Change News*, the World Meteorological Organization tweeted, "Too much, too fast." Later that summer, Greenland had its highest temperature ever for the month of June. In 2016, the Arctic region as a whole saw its ice shrink to the second-lowest record levels.

The year before, a team of US scientists began a three-year project to more accurately measure Greenland's ice melt. Some of the ice melt comes from icebergs that break off the island and drift into the ocean. The rest happens on Greenland's surface. The scientists already knew that the melting ice created lakes, which then fed new rivers that melted more ice. Lawrence Smith, the head of the research team, said the rivers melt the ice "like a knife through butter." The water then flows through holes in the ice sheets and eventually reaches the ocean, adding to the sea level rise. Smith and his team hope their measurements will help determine just how much the seas could rise through the rest of this century.

The increasingly fast melting of Arctic sea ice does not just affect ocean levels. The loss of ice seems to shape how ocean currents flow and influence weather patterns in the atmosphere.

The results of several studies published in 2016 suggest that melting sea ice can create what is called blocking. Earth's weather is affected by changes in air pressure above the planet's surface. Low-pressure systems are associated with storms, while high-pressure systems bring clear skies and calmer weather. In summer, the highs are sometimes the cause of heat waves.

The air pressure forces warm air near the surface to stay there, rather than rise up into the atmosphere. With blocking, a high-pressure system might sit above one region for many days or even several weeks. When blocking occurs over Greenland, more ice melts than usual. Using weather data going back to 1851, scientists saw that over the last 30 years, blocking was happening over Greenland more often, particularly during the warm summer months.

How does melting sea ice seem to increase the odds of blocking, leading to more melting? Jennifer Francis of Rutgers University was part of a team of scientists who studied this. As Francis explained to the *Washington Post* in 2016, with less ice on the ocean, it has a darker surface and so absorbs more of the sun's heat, especially in the late spring and summer. "And so the surface of the ocean…warms up quite a bit, and that extra heat is then also transferred into the atmosphere." In the atmosphere, the extra heat affects the **jet stream**. The change in the jet stream from the increased heat in the Arctic creates the blocking pattern that adds to the warmer temperatures.

The cycle of warming that melts ice, which then creates conditions for more warming—and more melting—is sometimes called Arctic **amplification**. This amplification explains why temperatures in the Arctic are rising faster than in other parts of Earth. Arctic amplification's effects on the jet stream could worsen in the coming years. Temperature differences between the Arctic and lower **latitudes** above the Equator are shrinking. If that continues, the jet stream could slow down, which would lead to greater swings north and south in the pattern it follows. When the jet stream takes a more northerly path, it allows warmer air from the southern latitudes to work its way over the Arctic, further increasing temperatures there.

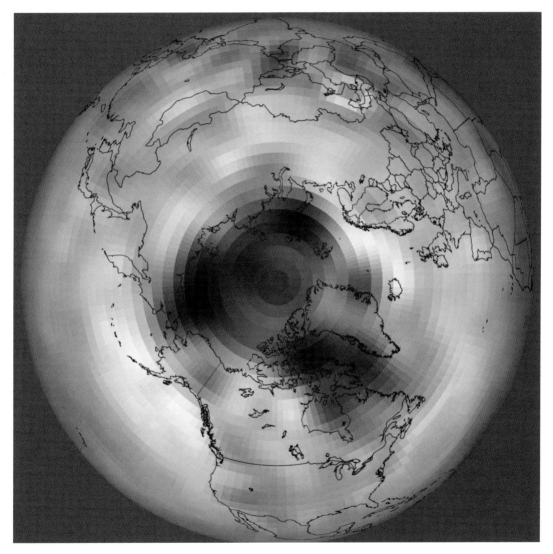

This diagram from NASA shows the change in average temperature from 2001 to 2011 at the northern polar region. The darkest red bands show a 7°F/–13°C increase.

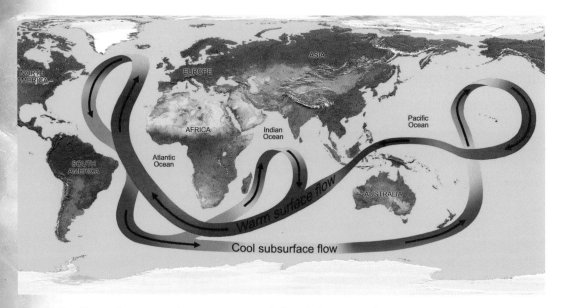

Trace the flow of water as it moves around the globe to see how it changes temperature from place to place. This circulation needs to work right for global seas to be healthy.

Scientists documented that in 2015, the jet stream moved farther north than usual, and that summer northwestern Greenland saw a record ice melt. The shift in the jet stream is most likely caused by Arctic amplification. The amplification is ongoing, so scientists think more record ice melts will occur over the next decade.

Changing Ocean Currents

Climate change in the Arctic may also be affecting how Earth's ocean currents move. The shifting of warm and cold water around the planet by these currents influences the climate. One of the most important current systems for Earth's climate is called the

Atlantic Meridional Overturning Circulation (AMOC). Among other things, this system moves heat from the Southern Hemisphere to the north. In 2015, some scientists feared that ice melt in Greenland was slowing down the AMOC, which could result in cooler winters and summers in the North Atlantic. The change could also raise sea levels along the east coast of North America. The AMOC moves because of the differences in the density of cold and warm salt water. The freshwater from the Arctic ice reduces that difference, adding less-dense water to the ocean and potentially slowing down the current.

Scientists, however, do not fully understand how the ocean currents affect weather on a global scale. Not all were ready to say that Greenland's ice melt was impacting the AMOC, since the current system was slowing down even before the recent massive ice melts. Natural changes, such as more rainfall in the Arctic or just normal variations in its movement, could also be playing a role.

The Cold Blob

While most of Earth was experiencing record heat during 2015, scientists were puzzled by a particularly cold spot in the North Atlantic Ocean just south of Greenland. The area of record-low temperatures came to be called the "cold blob," and it was about half the size of the United States. Several climate scientists suggested it resulted from the slowing of the AMOC. Michael Mann of Penn State said global warming was slowing the current enough to create the blob. Scientist Stefan Rahmstorf of Germany agreed and told the *Washington Post*, "I do expect the AMOC to decline further in the coming decades. The accelerated melting of the Greenland ice sheet will continue to contribute to this decline…" In 2016, Dutch scientists asserted that the blob resulted from unusually cold winter air in 2014–15 cooling the surface water in a part of the Atlantic called the Irminger Sea. These scientists rejected the notion that Greenland ice melt was the cause. Still, climate scientists such as Mann and Rahmstorf worry that the climate change and ice melt will affect the AMOC.

The Melting Ground

Scientists do see climate change as the source of another major change in the Arctic. Most of the region has a layer of soil just below the surface that always remains frozen, and has been for thousands of years. Known as permafrost, it contains grasses and bones from ancient animals as well as soil. Across the tundra, permafrost has provided a solid foundation on which people build roads and buildings. But warming in the Arctic is causing the permafrost to melt.

Trapped in the permafrost across the region are large amounts of carbon. Scientists estimate that the permafrost holds twice as much carbon as what is currently in the atmosphere. As the frozen soil melts, some of the carbon stored in it enters the atmosphere in the form of the greenhouse gases CO_2 and methane. The melting permafrost also creates new lakes, and the softening ground causes trees and even homes to lean. The new lakes cause even more permafrost to melt. Permafrost beneath existing lakes is melting too, and the carbon locked into the soil there is more likely to be turned into methane, which can increase warming more than CO_2. In 2015, several research scientists predicted that the release of greenhouse gases from melting permafrost could also have a huge economic effect. Such things as the destruction of cities from rising waters and the loss of crops could cost the world's nations trillions of dollars by the year 2200.

The melting permafrost shows Arctic amplification at work again. Warming in the Arctic results in changes in the environment that produce more greenhouse gases, and so increase global warming. Ted Schuur, a researcher at Northern Arizona State University, studies the effects of forest fires on permafrost.

An Arctic hare stands up for a better view of what's coming, which will probably include a warming of the permafrost region in which the animals live.

Ongoing weather pattern changes have helped lead to an increase in forest fires, which leads to a faster melting of the permafrost.

Forest fires in part of Canada and Alaska have increased in recent years, and that also contributes to the permafrost's melting. Schuur told the *Washington Post* in 2016 that the information he saw that year said that carbon is escaping the permafrost "several times faster even than our previous measurements have told us."

Text-Dependent Questions:

1. How is the melting of permafrost one example of Arctic amplification?

2. What role does blocking seem to play in warming the temperature in Greenland?

3. What is one natural occurrence in the oceans that could be affecting climate change?

 # Research Project

Find out what human activity produces the most emissions of greenhouse gases.

Melting ice news

Orcadas Base is run by the Scottish government on Laurie Island off the coast of Antarctica. Other nations have stations on the continent itself.

Antarctica and Climate Change

3

Unlike the Arctic, Antarctica remained a mystery to humans until the 19th century. While explorers saw southerly islands and giant icebergs, none actually spotted the continent until 1820, and it took until 1903 for a Scottish expedition to set up the first research station there. That station, called Ormond House, collected meteorological data. Already, scientists wanted to study the climate in the most hostile corner of the world. Ormond House is still in operation, though now it is under Argentine control.

Antarctica became a laboratory of sorts for studying climate change with Charles David Keeling's work measuring CO_2 in the atmosphere. The continent has also provided ice cores, and those samples are more reliable than the ones taken in Greenland for measuring past levels of CO_2. That's one reason why Antarctica is a crucial place for studying climate change, despite the difficulties of working there.

Antarctica has also been a key site for studying the **ozone** that makes up part of Earth's atmosphere. During the 1950s, scientists first noticed the ozone "hole." This is a wide area in the atmosphere above the South Pole from which the protective layer of ozone has been disappearing. This threatens to let in more dangerous solar rays the ozone would otherwise block. By the mid-1980s, scientists noticed the hole growing over Antarctica each year during the Southern Hemisphere's spring (the seasons are reversed there compared to North America). The ozone layer is important for all life on Earth, as it screens out harmful forms of **radiation** from the sun before they can reach Earth's surface.

Scientists have also learned that the increased radiation can affect the world's climate. One level of the atmosphere, the stratosphere, actually began cooling in the latter part of the 20th century. The cooling of the stratosphere over Antarctica, because of the ozone hole, has affected weather patterns around the continent and beyond. In Antarctica, the ozone hole has kept the region from warming as fast as the Arctic, and kept East Antarctica from warming as fast as West Antarctica. Globally, scientists have seen changing wind patterns and an increase in humidity in some tropical regions.

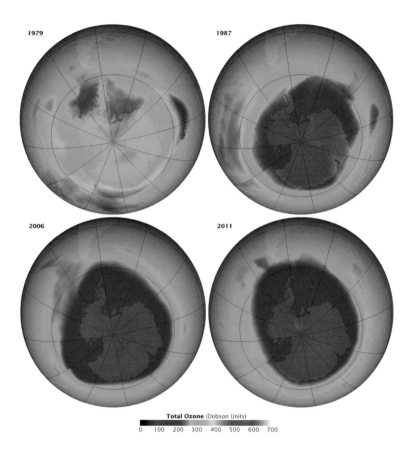

Though the growth is now slowing, this chart shows how rapidly the ozone hole over Antarctica grew from the late 1970s to recent years.

Scientists also think that increased radiation reaching Earth could play a role in promoting global warming. The radiation, along with other factors, can increase the release of greenhouse gases from plants and the soil. For some sea life, climate change and increased radiation combine to pose a deadly threat. The rising levels of CO_2 cause levels of acid in the oceans to rise. The acid makes it harder for the sea life to produce the calcium

The Montreal Protocol As a Model?

The growing ozone hole over Antarctica presented a clear problem with a known cause. That made it easy, Professor Adrian Howkins argues, for the world to act quickly and sign the Montreal Protocol. The Paris Agreement of 2015 could be the start for a similar process when it comes to climate change, but there are differences. Howkins wrote in his 2016 book *The Polar Regions* that the world quickly found substances to replace the harmful CFCs. With climate change, "there is no technology in place that can immediately replace the abundant use of energy that currently comes from fossil fuels." Another problem is that some of the gases used to replace CFCs are adding to the greenhouse effect. In April 2015, the United States, Canada, and Mexico proposed changing the Montreal Protocol to limit the use if these replacement gases that could add to global warming.

they need to develop protective shells. Without that protection, they can be damaged by the radiation, which in turn makes it even harder for them to produce the calcium.

The story of the ozone hole over Antarctica, however, may have a happy ending. In 1987, most of the world's countries signed an agreement called the Montreal **Protocol**, which ended the use of gases called chlorofluorocarbons (CFCs). These gases were known to destroy the ozone layer, and they included the gases used in spray cans. In 2016, scientists saw the importance of eliminating the CFCs from the atmosphere. From its peak in 2000, the Antarctica ozone hole had shrunk by 1.5 million square miles (4 million sq km). While the hole does not shrink at a constant rate, the world is making progress in reducing the size of the hole for good. Susan Solomon, a professor at the Massachusetts Institute of Technology (MIT) who studies the ozone layer, told MIT News, "We can now be confident that the things we've done have put the planet on a path to heal." Tackling the problem of the growing ozone hole probably also helped slow the rate of global warming, as CFCs can add to the greenhouse effect.

More Melting Ice

While the story of preserving the ozone layer over Antarctica turned out well, climate change is presenting ongoing challenges. As in the Arctic, one of the biggest problems in Antarctica is

The seas around Antarctic are covered in winter months with sheet ice that slowly breaks up in summer; in recent years, that has been happening earlier and earlier.

melting ice and the threat of rising sea levels. For the past 50 years, scientists have noted that Antarctica has also experienced significant warming, and that in recent years that warming has been greater there than in most other parts of the planet. Scientists have also recorded high volumes of ice melt, though it has not been at the same level all across the continent.

In 2016, several scientists reported on the growing dangers associated with Antarctic ice melt. One study showed that the West Antarctic ice sheet was melting faster than expected. The

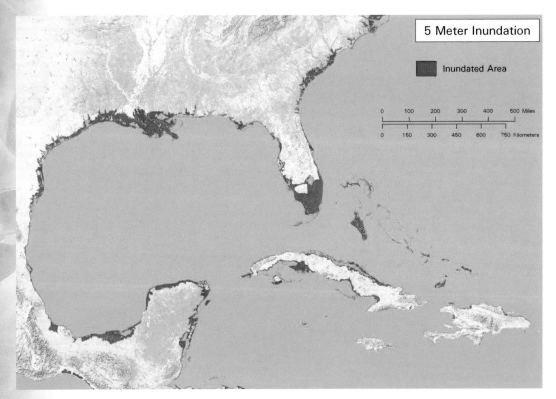

How much would a massive rise in sea level affect coastal communities? The red areas in this map would be underwater if sea level rose about 15 feet (5 m).

ice sheet is larger than Mexico, and scientists thought it could take hundreds or even thousands of years for it to melt. The study found that water from the ice sheet and other melting ice could cause ocean levels to rise by about 6 feet by the year 2100. Earlier studies thought a 3-foot rise was likely—enough to put the runways at several major US airports under water. A greater sea level rise would threaten to bring even more damage. Both warming air above the sheet and warming waters below it are contributing to the faster rate of melting. David Pollard of Pennsylvania State University took part in the study. He told *The New York Times* that scientists could not definitely say that the ice sheet would melt that quickly. "But I think we are pointing out that there's a danger, and it should receive a lot more attention."

Pollard and other researchers drew on data from the past, which showed that much warmer temperatures recorded 125,000 years ago caused global sea levels to rise by more than 30 feet (9.1 m). Then, they used computer models to work out how rising temperatures will affect the West Antarctic ice sheet today. The danger comes from smaller, floating sheets of ice that surround the larger West Antarctic sheet. They protect cliffs of ice on the larger sheet from summer melting. But if the smaller sheets melt, as they are, the larger ice sheet will be exposed to more melting. Something similar has already happened with some Greenland glaciers. The good news, Pollard said, is that if countries achieve

Antarctic glacier problems

Coming Sea Rise Disaster?

James Hansen was the NASA scientist who first made many Americans aware of the dangers of climate change associated with human activity. Since then, he has continued to study climate change, and in 2015 and 2016, he was often in the news as he predicted the world's seas could rise even faster because of polar ice melt.

He wrote a paper with several other scientists that spelled out the possible disasters unless there is a drastic cut in greenhouse gases. Hansen wrote that large amounts of ice could melt in a short time, and could raise sea levels much earlier than predicted. The paper also stressed that even the 3.6°F (2°C) temperature rise allowed for in the Paris Agreement is too high to stop the worst effects of climate change. Hansen's paper received criticism from other scientists. Some climate scientists thought Hansen's paper presented a worst-case situation not likely to happen. One said the odds of buying a winning multi-million dollar lottery ticket were almost as good.

the temperature goals spelled out in the 2015 Paris Agreement, the ice sheet will not melt as the models predicted.

Also in the west of Antarctica, on the peninsula, is an ice shelf that is drawing increased attention. An ice shelf is a large area of thick ice that floats on the water. Scientists have been watching a growing crack in the Larsen C ice shelf that stretches for 80 miles (128 km) and is more than 1,000 feet (305 m) wide. This crack could mean that a huge portion of the shelf will break off into the sea, as nearby ice shelves have already done. The area of ice likely to break off is about the size of the state of Delaware. One of the nearby shelves, Larsen B, almost disappeared completely, and scientists worry the same thing could happen to C. The loss of the ice shelf itself would not cause the ocean's waters to rise. But the shelf does keep glacial ice on land from pouring into the water. Without the shelf, the glacial ice would melt in the water and raise sea levels by several inches.

Check out this photo of the Totten Glacier while you can. Rising sea temperatures are rapidly shrinking this massive floe of ice.

On the other side of the continent, another 2016 report looked at the effect of the Totten Glacier melting. If global temperatures continued to rise at the same rate they have in recent years, the glacier would retreat almost 200 miles (321 km) inland. During that process, it would release enough water for ocean levels around the world to rise at least 6 feet (1.8 m). Currently, the surface of the glacier is thinning, losing about 1.5 feet (0.45 m) every year. With the Totten Glacier, warming sea water seems to be the main cause of the melt.

A Range of Temperatures

Overall, though, the waters around Antarctica have not warmed as much as Arctic waters. In 2016, scientists offered an explanation for this. Ocean currents constantly circulate water around the globe. The water off Antarctica is being pulled up from deep in the ocean, and that water has not been exposed to the atmosphere for hundreds or maybe a thousand years. Kyle Armour of the University of Washington led the study. He told *UW Today*, "The Southern Ocean is unique because it's bringing water up from several thousand meters." Water that has been warmed follows the ocean currents northward, and the water most affected by climate change reaches the Arctic, explaining the warmer waters recorded there. Armour said that this study points out that it may be more accurate to talk about regional warming rather than global warming.

That idea was supported by scientific work reported in 2015. Scientists had noticed that central Antarctica was not experiencing warming temperatures, as the rest of the continent and the planet were. The cause, researchers found, was that in that region, carbon dioxide has a negative greenhouse effect. Instead of keeping heat close to the planet's surface, the CO_2 lets it escape into the atmosphere. Physicist Justus Notholt of Germany and his team of scientists say the extremely cold temperatures on the surface of central Antarctica—the coldest on the planet—create this effect. Little heat from CO_2 rises from the ground there into the stratosphere. Normally, CO_2 in the stratosphere absorbs heat in the atmosphere and sends some into space and some back to Earth. Over the cold Antarctic, more of the warmth escapes than is sent back to Earth, meaning the surface does not warm.

Look closely and you'll see a fur seal basking in the sunshine on this small ice floe. The greenish color in the water also shows how much of such floes are submerged.

Scientists set up a weather measuring station. It can record temperature, wind speed, and precipitation and beam the results back to a research station.

Notholt's team reported that central Antarctica has even had a slight cooling of temperatures while the rest of the world has seen them increase.

The ice melt that is noticeable in some parts of Antarctica also does not happen the same everywhere on the continent. Some interior regions are seeing more snow than usual, which is adding to the amount of ice there. The added snow, however, is actually a sign of global warming across the planet. Antarctica normally receives little snow because the air is so dry; technically, the continent is considered a desert. But the rising temperatures on Earth are bringing more moisture to Antarctica, which means more snow.

NASA carried out the research that showed the ice levels are growing and released its results in 2015. Some scientists faulted the study, because some of the data NASA used was seven years old. A 2014 study using different data suggested the whole continent was losing ice. The NASA study and others reported around the same time showed the challenges climate scientists face as they try to accurately record the effects of global warming.

 # Text-Dependent Questions:

1. How might increased radiation reaching Earth's surface add to global warming?

2. Melting ice from the West Antarctic ice sheet could raise the ocean's waters by how much by 2100?

3. Why does scientist Adrian Howkins think it will be harder for the world to limit greenhouse gases than it was to eliminate the use of the gases that created the ozone hole?

 # Research Project

The map on page 40 shows how sea level rise would affect Florida, Mexico, and the Caribbean. Do some research and make a map of how sea level rise might affect Europe.

Huge, powerful ships like this icebreaker can crush through the ice-covered seas of the polar regions, opening new sea lanes but bringing new problems.

Opportunity and Challenges

4

Words to Understand

erode   wash away material such as soil, because of moving water

icebreakers   ships specially built to sail through icy waters and clear a path for other ships

multidisciplinary   combining several different fields of science to study a problem

Northwest Passage   a sea route through the Arctic Ocean that connects the Atlantic and Pacific Oceans

While melting ice sheets present problems for the entire world, climate change could have a few positive effects for some people in the Arctic.

In Russia, for example, the warming climate allows large ships to sail what is called the Northern Sea Route. Taking this route, a ship can sail from Europe to Asia about twice as fast than if it took the usual path through Egypt's Suez Canal. Most ships use the route, however, to go from one Arctic port to another. Russia also plans to use it to bring natural resources it takes from the

Arctic to international ports. In 2015, more than five million tons of cargo sailed on the route, most of it going from one Russian port to another. The Northern Sea Route, however, still presents challenges to shipping. It's only open about five months during the year, July to November, and in some places many ships still need **icebreakers** traveling with them. Experts think the Arctic will have to warm even more before more ships take the route. And even then, the region's harsh weather and remote location poses risks. In 2014, a South Korean fishing ship sank in the Bering Sea, which is just south of the Arctic Circle. The nearest rescue ship was almost 600 miles (965 km) away when the accident happened.

The natural resources that Russia moves out of the Arctic are becoming easier to reach because of global warming. Russian and international companies increasingly have access to new sources of minerals, oil, and natural gas. A 2008 study by the US government said that more than 20 percent of world's oil and gas yet to be discovered is north of the Arctic Circle. Most of these fossil fuels are found offshore. Russia opened the first offshore oil platform in the Arctic in 2013.

Still, working in the harsh Arctic climate is difficult, with oil workers and miners facing temperatures well below zero. At a Canadian gold mine, temperatures reached −40°F/°C, causing steel beams to crack. Drilling for oil in the region also presents problems. In parts of Russia, companies have already spilled several million barrels of oil on land. If the oil is spilled into water,

The oil pipelines that crisscross areas of the Arctic Circle bring vital fuel to many countries, but a spill from them would be disastrous.

cleaning it up will be hard because of the extreme temperatures. And while global warming is bringing more exploration for and removal of natural resources, it presents its own problems. The pipes that carry oil over land are built on permafrost, and many large trucks roll along on roads made of ice. Rising temperatures melt the permafrost and the roads, making it harder to transport goods and people.

The town that went under: The entire village of Shishmaref, Alaska, is closing up. Residents voted to move rather than be ruined by encroaching seas.

Changes for the Arctic Peoples

For the Arctic's indigenous people, climate change presents a few positive changes and many challenges. For some Inuit of northern Canada, the extracting of natural resources provides jobs they never had before. Linda Avatituq drives a truck for a mining company. She told *National Geographic* in 2016, "My life changed after I got the job...I can support my family and my grandkids." In Greenland, earlier and warmer summers mean people can grow crops and herbs that would not grow before. In the wild, more plants mean that reindeer get fatter, providing better-tasting game for indigenous hunters.

But for many indigenous people, global warming is not a blessing. Melting sea ice means hunters can't take the paths they did in the past to find game. In some places, the animals are moving northward to escape the warming, making it harder for the hunters to reach them. In northern Europe, reindeer herds have shrunk because warming temperatures have brought more rain, which makes it hard for the animals to reach lichen, an important part of the reindeer's diet. The changing climate can also affect where people live. In 2016, residents of the mostly indigenous village of Shishmaref, Alaska, voted to relocate their entire town from its island site to the mainland. The reason: In recent years, powerful storms have caused the island to **erode**. Rising temperatures have melted sea ice that once protected the coastline from the storms. Melting permafrost also makes the land more vulnerable to erosion.

Global warming is also raising the risk of forest fires in parts of the Arctic. In 2007, part of Alaska's tundra experienced its first wildfire in thousands of years, sparked by lightning. Warming temperatures that dry out the ground and lower levels of rain and snow let the fire spread. By 2015, the situation was even worse, with hundreds of wildfires erupting across the state, burning millions of acres. Some blazes start in areas so remote that firefighters don't even realize they're burning. The fires, in turn, melt the permafrost, releasing the greenhouse gases stored in them and increasing Arctic amplification. One Alaska scientist told the *Washington Post*, "Everything's connected. The climate, the permafrost, the water, the fires. You can't look at one thing without looking at another. Changes in one changes everything else."

Selawik, Alaska, is one of many small towns and villages whose residents are dealing with climate change effects on their traditional ways of life.

In parts of the Arctic, the effects of climate change are also disrupting the traditional indigenous ways of life. As more Inuit take jobs in mining, some people in their communities worry that their children will not learn how to hunt traditional game. A warming climate could also kill off plants and animals that are an important part of indigenous art and religion. Even efforts to slow global warming by turning away from fossil fuels can affect the local people. In parts of Arctic Europe, companies have set up wind farms in Sami territories. The farms have destroyed lands where reindeer grazed.

Tourism in the Polar Regions

Global warming in the polar regions also presents both opportunities and challenges connected to tourism. In the Arctic in 2016, a large cruise ship sailed through the **Northwest Passage**. The *Crystal Serenity* carried 1,700 passengers and crew on its trip from Alaska to New York. Along the way, the ship stopped at several small Inuit villages, giving residents a chance to earn money by selling

The Role of Drones

As global warming changes the environment, scientists are turning to drones for several important missions. The small, radio-controlled devices can provide a close look at endangered animals, such as sea lions and ice seals, in the polar regions. The drones can record if a species population is falling. With wildfires, a drone can safely fly beyond the smoke and detect where the fire is at its worst or where it could spread. Firefighters can then target those areas. In the future, drones could be used to measure changes to the coastline as global warming continues or they could take part in search-and-rescue missions as more ships sail off Alaska's coast. Drones have also been used to help icebreakers create safe lanes to reach Antarctic research stations.

arts and crafts to the tourists. Some Inuit also saw the visits as a way to educate the passengers about their traditional lifestyle.

But the voyage worried some safety experts, who noted the difficulty of sailing such a large ship through narrow passages that could still contain sea ice, even during the summer. The *Crystal Serenity* could also face severe weather. The ship's owner added extra technology to look for ice and hired an icebreaker to sail with the cruise liner. It carried two helicopters that were also used to scout for ice.

Some environmentalists worry about the impact of large ships on a mostly unspoiled natural area already facing changes from climate change. John Hocevar of the group Greenpeace told the *New York Times*, "polar bears, ice seals, walruses are literally fighting for survival. This is no time to be adding additional stresses to such a sensitive situation."

Tourism is increasing in Antarctica as well, with some similar issues arising. Between 35,000 and 45,000 tourists come to the continent each summer, with the largest number coming from the United States. While that seems like a fairly small number, more people are interested in going there, and scientists aren't sure what kind of impact they could have on the wildlife and land in the future. The International Maritime Organization introduced rules to try to limit the effects of tourism. These include limiting the number of people who can come ashore at one time to 100, having tourists stay back from penguins, and requiring ships to use cleaner fuels.

Human activity is already having an effect on some sea life near Antarctica, because of global warming. Krill are tiny creatures that look like shrimp and are an important source of food for whales and other sea life. Fishermen also catch krill to use as food at commercial fish farms. But studies by So Kawaguchi of Australia suggest that the krill population of the Southern

Local residents wave to visiting tourists: The arrival of cruise ships to sensitive Antarctic areas has been very controversial.

Scientists fear that Adélie penguins like these, who depend on sea ice for safety and breeding grounds, could be in danger with rising sea temperatures.

Ocean could fall if global warming puts more CO_2 into the ocean, as it is already doing. He told *The New York Times*, "If we continue with business as usual, and we don't act on reducing carbon emissions, there could be a 20 to 70 percent reduction in Antarctic krill by 2100."

On land, a warming Antarctica is already affecting some penguins. Changes in the ocean are killing off some of the fish they eat. Loss of sea ice particularly affects Adélie penguins, who live on the ice in winter. In 2016, scientists predicted that Adélie and emperor penguins could face huge population declines through the 21st century. Still, given the uneven impact of climate change on the continent, some penguin colonies could survive.

What Lies Ahead

Scientists realize the potential for climate change to impact the whole planet. The polar regions, though, show what can happen where the warming is its most extreme. The changes go beyond those regions to affect many parts of the world. Adrian Howkins wrote in *The Polar Regions* that those regions "have become central to the science and politics of global climate change… if taken seriously, images of collapsing glaciers, graphics of shrinking Arctic ice, and

Locked in Ice

If all goes well, Matthew Shupe and a team of other scientists will spend a year on a ship locked into Arctic ice. Shupe and his team are planning a project called the **Multidisciplinary** drifting Observatory for the Study of the Arctic—MOSAic for short. The scientists want to measure what happens below, on, and above the ice pack during the year, and especially during the winter. Normally, scientists stop their research in the Arctic during the extreme winter cold. But the MOSAic team will take their ship into the ocean during the fall and wait for the waters around them to freeze. Then the ship will float along in the ice and the scientists can take their measurements. One thing Shupe wants to study is how clouds might affect global warming in the Arctic. Do the clouds trap more heat close to the surface, or do they block out the sun from heating it? This mission comes after researchers from Norway already locked a ship into Arctic ice, but MOSAic is a much larger project. If all goes as planned, Shupe and the others will begin their research in 2019.

Limited tourism, it is hoped, will be a long-term benefit. If people witness these pristine areas first hand, they might become defenders of the land and its wildlife.

statistics for dying penguins and polar bears cannot help but cause despair." Slowing or even halting the increasing temperatures in the polar regions will shape what the Arctic and Antarctica look like decades from now—and the rest of the world as well.

Text-Dependent Questions:

1. What is one possible benefit of global warming for indigenous people of the Arctic?

2. How do forest fires in the Arctic add to the emission of greenhouse gases?

3. Why does Matthew Shupe want to study the affect of clouds on the Arctic during the winter?

 # Research Project

Go online to find the most recent information you can on how much Arctic or Antarctic ice has melted in the past few years.

Antarctic ice and wildlife

FIND OUT MORE

Websites

Antarctica
www.cia.gov/library/publications/resources/the-world-factbook/geos/ay.html

The Arctic – WWF Global
wwf.panda.org/what_we_do/where_we_work/arctic/

Climate Change: Basic Information
www3.epa.gov/climatechange/basics/

Climate Change in the Arctic
nsidc.org/cryosphere/arctic-meteorology/climate_change.html

The Emerging Arctic
www.cfr.org/polar-regions/emerging-arctic/p32620#!/?cid=otr_marketing_use-arctic_Infoguide

Polar Regions
www.seeker.com/tag/polar-regions#news.discovery.com.

Books

Arnéz, Lynda. *Native Peoples of the Arctic.* New York: Gareth Stevens Publishing, 2017.

Bow, James. *Earth's Climate Change: Carbon Dioxide Overload.* New York: Crabtree Publishing Company, 2015.

Feinstein, Stephen. *Critical Perspectives on Climate Change.* New York: Enslow Publishing, 2017

Mara, Wil. *Antarctica.* New York: Children's Press, 2017.

 SERIES GLOSSARY OF KEY TERMS

circumpolar: the area surrounding the North Pole, including the Arctic regions

Cold War: when nations are openly hostile toward each other while not resorting to physical warfare

continental shelf: the relatively shallow seabed surrounding a continent; the edge of a continent as it slopes down into the sea

floe: an ice sheet floating in the water

indigenous: native or original to a particular place

meteorology: the study of weather

pelts: furred animal skins

permafrost: a layer of soil that stays frozen all year long

province: an area in Canada with its own name and government, similar to a state

subsistence: a basic, minimal way of living, with only things that are necessary to survive

sustainable: something that can be maintained or practiced for a long duration without negative effects

taiga: a biome that includes the forest of mostly evergreen trees found in the southern Arctic regions

territorial waters: the parts of an ocean over which a country has control

tundra: a type of biome in very cold areas characterized by limited plant growth, frozen soil, and low rainfall

INDEX

PHOTO CREDITS

123RF: Leonid Ikan 51. Adobe Images: Achim Baqué 6, Daulon 11, Jean-Jacques Cordier 15, staphy 16, Andrew Watson 20, mrallen 24, Adwo 31, Mtphotostock 32, Silver 39, Kovalenko 48, Doethion 57, B201735 60. Bering Land Bridge National Conservancy: 52. CRESIS: 40. Dreamstime.com: Andrey Salamchev 18, Timwege 45, ndp 58. Independent: 43. Newscom: John Angelilli/UPI 23, Bob Hallinen/MCT 54. NASA/JPL: 28, 32. NOAA: 27, Naraynese/Semu 12. NSF/Antarctic Photo Library: 46. NSIDC: Scambos and Bauer 13.

ABOUT THE AUTHOR

Michael Burgan has written more than 250 books for children and teens, as well as newspaper articles and blog posts. Although not an athlete, he has written on both amateur and professional sports, including books on the Basketball Hall of Fame, the Olympics, and great moments in baseball. And although not a medical professional, he regularly writes web content on a variety of health topics. He lives in Santa Fe, New Mexico with his cat Callie.